Beyond Silence
Revealing Ourselves

Preface

I have been wrestling with a truth that has evaded me for years. My dearest friend, Dr. Vanessa Harris, a woman of wisdom and grace, has long urged me to write. She believes in the power of words to heal the wounds we carry. "A Father's Footsteps" was a tentative step in that direction. I crafted it with the questions I imagined my children, grandchildren, or perhaps some future kin might ask. "What was Kyle like? Tell me about him." Unasked and unanswered, these questions linger in the silence because no one thought to inquire, and I never dared to reveal.

Since embarking on this literary journey, a new urge has taken root—a compulsion to share my essence. Among my family, I have come to realize my uniqueness. This uniqueness is neither a blessing nor a curse; it simply is. Yet, I still grapple with the courage to pen the narrative of my soul. Instead, I will fill this book, hoping it will offer some glimpse into the man I am.

After I published "A Father's Footsteps," Dr. Harris enlightened me about its profound impact. She spoke of the countless men separated from their children by duty, distance, or circumstance—be they military personnel, expatriates, or even those incarcerated-who yearn to leave a piece of themselves behind. This book is for those who wish to bridge the chasm of absence and share their truths with those who matter.

This is for the ones close to your heart, not just your children, but anyone with whom you desire to share your story. As you fill these pages, be truthful. We are not saints, but our stories, in all their flawed beauty, deserve to be told. Enjoy this journey of self-discovery and revelation; pass it on to those you love when the time comes.

In the end, may this book serve as a testament to the power of vulnerability and the courage it takes to be seen. In sharing who we are, we find connection; in connection, we find our place in the world.

K.H

Table of Contents

Defining Moments and Identity..3

Love and Relationships 7

Dreams and Aspirations 13

Pain and Growth...18

Values and Beliefs 25

Experiences and Stories 29

Personal Growth and Self-Care 35

Personal Reflection and Philosophy...51

Inspirational and Motivational...57

Emotions and Mental Well-being..61

Defining Moments and Identity

1. What are the defining moments in your life that shaped your sense of self?

2. What are the aspects of your identity that you cherish the most?

3. What are the qualities you appreciate most in yourself?

4. How do you reconcile your individual identity with your role in the family?

5. What are the experiences that have shaped your identity?

6. How do you navigate the complexities of identity and belonging?

7. What memories do you cherish the most from your childhood?

8. What are the qualities you strive to embody?

Love and Relationships

9. How do you express love, and how do you wish to receive it?

10. Can you recount a time when someone truly understood you? What was that experience like?

11. How do you show love and appreciation to others?

12. How do you handle feelings of envy or jealousy within your family dynamics?

13. How do you set and maintain boundaries in your relationships?

14. What are the qualities you admire most in others?

15. What are the qualities you seek in your friendships and relationships?

16. What are the moments of connection that you treasure the most?

17. How do you navigate feelings of loneliness or isolation?

18. What are the friendships that have shaped you the most?

19. What are the qualities you value most in your relationships?

20. How do you approach conflicts with loved ones?

Dreams and Aspirations

21. What dreams do you hold dear but have never shared with anyone?

22. What are the dreams that you are currently pursuing?

23. What dreams have you let go of, and why?

24. How do you define and pursue happiness?

25. What are the experiences that have made you feel most alive?

26. How do you find a balance between ambition and contentment?

27. How do you approach the idea of legacy, and what do you want to leave behind?

28. What are the challenges you face in pursuing your dreams?

29. How do you cultivate a sense of adventure in your life?

Pain and Growth

30. How have your experiences of pain influenced your outlook on life and relationships?

31. How do you cope with feelings of loneliness or isolation?

32. How do you navigate feelings of being shunned or misunderstood by your family?

33. How do you handle rejection, and what have you learned from it?

34. How do you deal with unmet expectations and disappointments?

35. How do you handle feelings of guilt or shame?

36. How do you deal with feelings of inadequacy or self-doubt?
_____
_____
_____
_____
_____
_____
_____
_____
_____
_____
_____
_____
_____
_____
_____
_____
_____
_____

37. How do you navigate feelings of regret or remorse?
_____
_____
_____
_____
_____
_____
_____
_____
_____
_____
_____
_____
_____
_____
_____
_____
_____
_____

38. How do you handle feelings of resentment or anger?

39. How do you handle feelings of fear or uncertainty?

40. How do you handle feelings of sadness or grief?

41. What lessons have you learned from your most challenging experiences?

42. How do you navigate the complexities of family loyalty and personal autonomy?

43. How do you navigate the complexities of familial expectations?

Values and Beliefs

44. What are the values that guide your decisions and actions?

45. How do you stay true to yourself despite external pressures?

46. How do you stay grounded in your values and beliefs?

47. What are the beliefs or philosophies that guide your life?

48. How do you define success, and how has that definition evolved over time?

49. How do you approach the idea of success and failure?

50. What are the values that you hold most dear?

Experiences and Stories

51. What are the books, films, or artworks that resonate deeply with you?

52. What small joys bring light to your everyday life?

53. What memories bring you the most comfort and why?

54. What stories do you want to be remembered from your life?

55. What are the moments of courage that you are proud of?

___

56. What are the moments of kindness that have touched you deeply?

___

57. What are the moments of joy that you hold dear?

58. What are the moments of connection that you hold dear?

59. What are the experiences that have brought you the most growth?

60. What are the experiences that have brought you the most joy?

61. What are the experiences that have shaped your worldview?

62. What are the moments of kindness that have inspired you?

Personal Growth and Self-Care

63. How do you balance your personal desires with the expectations of others?

64. How do you manage stress and anxiety in your daily life?

65. How do you find peace amidst chaos and conflict?

66. How do you practice self-compassion and kindness towards yourself?

67. How do you cultivate resilience and perseverance?

68. How do you nurture your mental and emotional well-being?

69. How do you practice gratitude in your daily life?

70. What are the ways in which you practice self-care?

71. How do you maintain hope in the face of adversity?

_____
_____
_____
_____
_____
_____
_____
_____
_____
_____
_____
_____
_____
_____
_____
_____

72. How do you cultivate a sense of purpose in your life?

_____
_____
_____
_____
_____
_____
_____
_____
_____
_____
_____
_____
_____
_____
_____
_____

73. How do you find meaning in your everyday life?

74. How do you navigate the challenges of change and transition?

75. How do you approach personal growth and development?

76. How do you stay true to your values and beliefs?

Connection and Community

77. How do you wish your family would perceive and understand you?

78. What are the unspoken rules in your family that have affected you?

79. How do you show love and appreciation to others?

80. How do you contribute to your community?

81. How do you navigate the balance between vulnerability and strength?
___

82. How do you balance the need for solitude with the need for connection?
___

83. How do you cultivate a sense of belonging and community?

84. How do you navigate feelings of loneliness or isolation?

Creativity and Expression

85. How do you express your creativity, and what mediums do you prefer?

86. What are the hobbies or activities that bring you joy?

87. How do you nurture your creativity?

88. How do you show love and appreciation to others?

89. How do you find beauty in everyday life?

90. How do you find peace in moments of turmoil?

91. What are the rituals or routines that ground you?

92. How do you approach making difficult decisions?

93. How do you maintain a sense of wonder and curiosity?

Personal Reflection and Philosophy

94. How do you reconcile your individual identity with your role in the family?

95. How do you navigate the tension between tradition and innovation?

96. How do you cultivate a sense of belonging and community?

97. How do you find balance in your life?

98. What lessons have you learned from your successes and failures?

99. How do you approach personal growth and development?

100. How do you cultivate a sense of purpose and direction in your life?

101. How do you find meaning in your everyday life?

102. How do you handle feelings of disappointment or frustration?

103. How do you navigate the complexities of love and relationships?

104. How do you navigate the complexities of family dynamics?

Inspirational and Motivational

105. What are the sources of inspiration and motivation in your life?

106. How do you stay grounded in your values and beliefs?

107. How do you maintain a sense of hope and optimism?

108. What are the moments of courage that have defined you?

109. What are the lessons you wish to pass on to future generations?

110. How do you cultivate resilience and perseverance?

111. How do you handle feelings of fear or uncertainty?

112. How do you find balance in your life?

Emotions and Mental Well-being

113. How do you navigate feelings of guilt or regret?

114. How do you navigate feelings of loneliness or isolation?

115. How do you handle feelings of fear or uncertainty?

116. How do you deal with unmet expectations and disappointments?

117. How do you handle feelings of inadequacy or self-doubt?

_____
_____
_____
_____
_____
_____
_____
_____
_____
_____
_____
_____
_____
_____
_____
_____
_____

118. How do you manage stress and anxiety in your daily life?

_____
_____
_____
_____
_____
_____
_____
_____
_____
_____
_____
_____
_____
_____
_____
_____
_____

119. How do you handle feelings of resentment or anger?

120. How do you handle feelings of sadness or grief?

www.ingramcontent.com/pod-product-compliance
Lightning Source LLC
Chambersburg PA
CBHW050456110426
42743CB00017B/3386